MY LIFE
BY DESIGN

MY LIFE BY DESIGN

This journal belongs to:

MY LIFE BY DESIGN

The Ultimate Transformational Journal & Workbook

Created By
Kimberley Smith

This book was created and written by author and artist Kimberley Smith **www.kimberflydesign.com**.

Book design by Theresa McNeilly of **DoTheWorkBooks.com**.

Edited by Aura Fruitman.

Publication date: August, 2020.
Printed on acid-free paper.
Published by Kimberley Smith, Artist, Author and Consultant of Kimberfly Design and Young at Heart Painting.
Version 1.1
ISBN 978-1-7773470-0-0

Get in touch!
Website: **www.kimberflydesign.com**
Instagram: **@kimberflydesign**
Facebook: **kimberflydesign**
Email: **kimberflydesign@gmail.com**
Journal Club: **www.kimberflydesign.com**

What You All Mean to Me

My first book! Dedicated to my mother Beth—the strong, courageous, socially connected person to all people and things; my father Paul—my rock, respected business owner and my hero; my sister Lisa—who cares by helping her big sis, and keeps us all laughing; and my loving family and friends. You all continue to give me support and encouragement to go for my dreams. You answer the phone when I need your guidance; continue to give me advice; provide positive motivation that helps keep me moving forward - thank you. I am forever grateful.

Love love love you all!

Kimberley Smith

Dad and me

A Journaling Journey

As a young child, I took a keen interest in my Dad's creativity. I watched my father design, paint and illustrate. Inspired, I became an artist myself. Through drawing and designing, my sketch book became my 'art journal'. I would draw clothes I thought would be fun to wear, then I would sew them for friends. I realized how fulfilling this made me. Looking back, this was my first encounter with journaling. You write it down and it comes to life! A thought...a sketch...a stitch...a dress. Imagine that!

I have been journaling and setting goals for a few years now. It has made a significant impact in my life. Take this book for instance. I never thought that writing a book was possible, until of course I wrote it down in my journal. My wish is that you have a similar experience on your journaling journey. Do tell: **kimberflydesign@gmail.com**.

I hope you will find this book useful to help fulfil your dreams and live the life you have always desired.

Anything is possible!

With love and happiness,

Kimberley Smith

Visit **www.kimberflydesign.com** to download a free workbook tool kit.

Facebook: **kimberflydesign**

Instagram: **@kimberflydesign**

kimberflydesign@gmail.com

Become a member! Join the virtual journal club: **www.kimberflydesign.com**

Contents

What's inside?

Journal & Workbook Features

- 200-lined pages - to be filled with your hopes, dreams and aspirations!
- Over 20 insightful activities
- Different ways to manifest your dreams NOW - goal setting, gratitude, commitment, positive mindset, visualization, affirmations, positive language and accountability
- Journal prompts and quotes to keep you on track
- Hand-painted artwork
- Accomplishments Tracking Sheet

Why journal and how to get the most out of it

A journal is like a best friend - someone who is there for you, to listen and help guide you in the right direction. Journaling is a powerful tool that you use to transform and change things in your life for the better! The typical way people use journals is to write down stories and things that have happened. I am going to teach you how journaling can create the life you want and in turn, manifest your dreams. Journaling is a fun and neat way to dig deep and discover what you want in life.

Use your journal as a notebook. Write down notes, stories, hopes, aspirations and goals to help you grow in every area of your life. This will help you identify areas you want to improve. It will help you see what's important in your life, moving you forward into new possibilities. Now that's exciting!

I write in my journal daily. I use it to get things off my mind; write down my thoughts and feelings; note my successes for the day and develop lists of things I want to change.

Use your journal to write down things you want to work on, any dreams you may have. It can be anything, such as:

- » I want a new job
- » I want to move to a new house
- » I want to make more money so I can travel

Let your pen flow. Write down any and all thoughts that come to mind. Perhaps there is something not going as well as you would like in your life. Note it.

I focused on two specific areas: a better sales and marketing career, and to start my own learn-to-paint business. I watched YouTube videos, met with successful entrepreneurs, talked to friends - each time writing down what I learned in my—you got it—journal!

Ideas to Get You Journaling – Ready, Set, START!

- » a new job
- » future family goals
- » how much you want to save this year
- » where you want to travel
- » what kind of person you want to meet
- » the type of relationship you want with your partner, or family

Each week review your journal. Did you accomplish everything you said you would? Add those previous goals you didn't complete to a new page for the new day. This helps keep that goal present in your mind.

Every few months go back and read your journal from the beginning. Ask yourself: what has changed? What has happened? Have I met any of my goals? How many goals have I met?

When we reflect back on our goals, we can see how much we have done or not done. Keeping it "visually" present in your mind, **that's the magic!** Writing it down ensures

you 'see' it. Use the **Accomplishments Tracking Sheet** at the back of this book to record both your accomplishments and achievements.

That's the power of journaling!

You will be surprised what you will learn about yourself. You will eventually see how you are responsible for the design of your own life. Things will start happening. Don't be surprised if a few or more of your goals come to fruition! Let me know! Send me a message at **kimberflydesign@gmail.com**

#1 KimberTip: Refer to your lists and notes often - whenever you have a moment during the day or at night.

You can journal when and wherever you feel like it. The more you use it, the better results you will see. My journal is with me wherever I go, just in case I want to write something down.

Oh, and if you want to light a candle or sit with your favourite blanket—sip a cup of tea in the most quiet, coziest spot in your home—your journaling experience will be that much more enjoyable.

You can keep reading along, or feel free to jump right into it and start your first entry!

When do I start?

The beginning of your new **My Life By Design** began when you purchased this journal. Congratulations! Now it's time to grab your favourite pen and start writing!

How do I start?

10 Different ways of how you can use your journal:

Goals - Write down and list your goals for the day, the month, or the year. Dream up some big goals!

Details of Events - A journal is a great place to write down a good story of what happened during the day, so you can remember.

Help Process Thoughts and Feelings - Bad day? Write down all the details of the situation or event that happened. This can be very therapeutic!

To-Do List - Itemize what you have to do for the day or week.

Words of Affirmation - Words are powerful. Write down your affirmations to help manifest who you are and who you want to be.

School & Research - Taking a course or watching a lot of YouTube videos? Write down what you learn in your journal. A glance back at these 'learning notes' will awaken your recollection of information.

Brain Release - If you can't fall asleep at night, try to do a brain release. Write down everything that's worrying you in your journal before you fall asleep.

Gratitude - Write a list of things you are grateful for. By acknowledging gratitude, your mindset changes to a more positive state. Empowered, you are more driven to meet your goals.

Ideas - We are always coming up with new ideas and thoughts. Write your ideas down so you don't lose or forget them.

Celebrate - Always take time to celebrate YOU. List successes that make you feel proud. Recognize and appreciate all you have done.

#2 KimberTip: Remember to always date your entry.

Activity #1 - I use this journal to/for...

What do you want to get out of journaling? Think about why you purchased this journal and write it down here.

Example: *I, Kimberley, use this journal to.... fast track my personal transformation and goal setting. I also use it to record and track daily tasks and accomplishments.*

I use this journal to/for...

Who Am I?

The Power Behind The Pen

My first journal

Four months into my new job as an Account Executive at a corporate marketing firm in a very prestigious downtown area of Toronto, Canada, I recall not being happy. My direct supervisor would ask: "how are you doing?" In a small quiet voice I would respond with a complete full-out lie: "I'm fine", when in fact, I really wasn't fine at all.

I felt desperate, unfocused and extremely unmotivated. I was lost. What was I doing there? How did I get there? Anxiety set in as I questioned - how do I leave this job? Where do I go? Do I quit and find another job in the same industry? Now what?

I said to myself, let me find out if there is any help out there. I shared my struggles with my friend Missy. Missy introduced me to Tom Walters who said he could help me! He requested that I bring a journal to our first meeting. "Journaling? You can ask me to draw or paint you a picture, sure, but journaling? I hate writing." I was skeptical.

Like I said, I was desperate. I decided to give up all of "what I thought I knew" and do it anyway. At our initial meeting he brought out his leather folder with sheets of paper bound together. And tons of handwritten notes. I brought out my first blue journal, blank pages in sharp contrast.

We sat at a table with two small chairs on the second floor of this quaint coffee house in downtown Toronto. The upstairs was tiny, packed with people and yet, peacefully quiet. With other book worms, people studying and listening to their headphones, Tom started to share his thoughts about journaling. He told me he writes everyday for the following reasons:

- for a positive well-being
- to manage emotions
- to neutralize distractive thoughts
- to increase the benefits of meditation practice
- to foster creativity

And for long term goals, he uses the journal:

- to clear space in the mind to recognize new and interesting knowledge
- to collect thoughts and data for presentations and future publication opportunities

I am grateful for that first encounter that led me on my journaling journey to success.

Manifest Your Dreams

I'm sharing what tools to use to manifest your dreams because I believe this to be my truth, my experience. And it's okay if you have never journaled before. Many haven't. The magic is transferring - your thoughts to pen and paper. Look, review, keep it fresh in your consciousness. That's how it gets manifested.

How many times have you heard someone say (or perhaps you have said it yourself), "Oh, if only I had this, then I would do that." Did anything come of this statement? We all talk like this. Put your talk into action. Write it down. See what happens.

That's how I started my own business, in 2018, called Young at Heart Painting. Since then the company has served over 5,000 seniors and their families. This all started by writing it down. This all started by writing down my thoughts and ideas on paper.

I also eliminated my debt! Journaling is the tool I used to help me deal with and eliminate years of debt and start an investment portfolio. Talk about manifesting your dreams. This works!

Manifest **your** dreams. Journaling will keep you motivated by creating a new positive mindset. And heck, it's super fun!

Activity #2 - What's your story?

Now it's your turn. Who are you? What's your story?

7 Areas of Life

Goals for a fantastic life!

There are many areas of life which you may want to work on in your journal. Below are 7 key areas. You might start with a goal you already have in mind or a particular area of life that isn't working that well. For me it was my career and romantic relationships.

#3 KimberTip: Make a list of qualities and desirable traits you want in your romantic partner. Be specific.

Activity #3 - What are your life goals?

Here is a space to write out your goals. In specific detail. Include: colours, sizes, areas, shapes, sounds, numbers. State a reasonable, attainable time frame. Review your goals daily. Once reached, set more goals. To start, circle the goals you want to focus on first.

Body *(health and fitness)*

Personal Development *(mind, emotions, psychology and beliefs)*

Relationships *(social/friends/fun/romantic)*

Family

Business/Career

Money/Finances

Spirituality *(religion, meditation practice)*

Activities to Manifest Your Dreams

Gratitude

In today's busy world, we are so caught up with what we want and where we want to go, that we forget and neglect what we have right now in the moment.

At some point in your life you wanted the car you are currently driving or the home you are currently living in. Take the time to be grateful for those things you currently have.

When we use gratitude, it helps us be more present and shifts our focus to a "positive and relaxed" state of mind. The results: you are empowered and driven to meet your goals listed.

» I am grateful for my creativity
» I am grateful I can drive
» I am grateful for my sister's support

#4 KimberTip: With practice and effort, your gratitude entries will evolve. From general to specific, with more meaning and insight.

Activity #4 - What are you grateful for?

Make a list of 10 things you are currently grateful for in your life. You can make a gratitude list daily or weekly.

1

2

3

4

5

6

7

8

9

10

Commitment

Ask yourself these questions: what have I agreed to? What am I dedicated to? What obligations do I have? Have I made a promise to someone or a pledge to do something?

And am I being true to myself, in 'action mode', carrying out my commitments? Stay motivated by following through; be loyal; be responsible. When your goals are supported through commitment, you are working toward creating your Life By Design!

#5 KimberTip: Honour your commitments. When you say you're going to do something, do it. And if not, question why. What do you fear?

Activity #5 - What am I committed to?

Before continuing...take a moment to write down what you are committed to. You can use this throughout your journaling. Keep writing things you are committed to. Be unreasonable. Think BIG!

For example: *I, Kimberley, am committed to taking one risk and action outside of my comfort zone, everyday. I am also committed to communicating supportive thoughts to my friends, creating an online business, and helping others live a happy fulfilled life.*

I am Committed to:

Positive Mindset

How do **you** deal with struggles in life? Journal it! Change your story. Change your mindset.

Can you think of a situation that you are currently struggling with? Your career? A family member? A friend? Your health? Do you feel you are unable to do something for some unknown reason? Maybe you are upset and frustrated and not taking action in that area of life.

#6 KimberTip: Focus on the good things, big or small.

Activity #6 - Write a Story

Take 10 minutes and describe your situation and how you feel about the struggle. Let your mind just flow. Talk about the incident. Write the impact it has on you. Keep writing and describing the event on the next page.

When you finish writing, go back and re-read your story. Take a moment and highlight all the facts about what happened.

Here is an example: *I live on my own and am so lonely. I'm always tired. I never feel like going out.*

Notice that the only factual information is: "I live on my own." We make up stories to our issues and attach a variety of emotions to it.

Listen to the stories in your head. Is it all true? Recognize and replace the untruths with true statements. Focus on real facts. This opens up space for you to think more clearly. And in turn, new ideas emerge, followed by new actions to take.

My Story

Visualization

Your mind is powerful. Visualizing a goal, picturing it in your mind, in detail, while feeling 'as if' the goal is happening right now, brings you closer to achieving it.

Practice visualizations daily in the morning and evening. Take your time. Stick with it.

#7 KimberTip: Find a calm space without distractions. Close your eyes and picture your 'wants'. Feel the feeling.

Activity #7 - A fun visualization exercise!

Each day, make a list of things you want. Concentrate on one thing at a time and imagine 'as if' you have it. What emotion comes up when you think of this new thing you want in your life? What does it look like? How does it feel? Practice this new feeling associated with this one thing. Once achieved, move on to your next goal.

Here are two examples:

What I want in my life	Describe the feeling of having it right now
A really great boyfriend	*I am happy, thrilled, fulfilled, excited, loved*
To travel more	*I am joyful, adventurous, awakened, satisfied*

What I want in my life	Describe the feeling of having it right now

Affirmations

An affirmation is a positive simple statement or declaration of who you are. When you affirm daily, you begin to believe in yourself. This 'better self' belief changes your thought patterns, attitude, and outlook on life.

#8 KimberTip: Post your affirmations where you will see them everyday: mirrors, bedside table, fridge, on the back of the front door.

Activity #8 - Write out your affirmations

Use positive language to write your affirmations. Stand in the moment and 'be' your affirmations, feel your new emotions. If you write: "I am powerful" - feel powerful. If you write: "I am courageous" - feel courageous. Other examples: **I am** kind, loving and *spontaneous.* **I am** *courageous and strong.*

1

2

3

4

5

6

7

8

9

10

11

12

Positive Language

Positive language equals positive thoughts. Did you know you have 70,000 thoughts per day and 70% of them are negative?

#9 KimberTip: Smile when you speak....even on the phone!

Activity #9 - The One-Two!

Hear the present conversations in your head; listen to the language you are using; acknowledge that they are there; adjust the wording to sound positive

One: write down all negative words you say.

Two: re-write the words or sentences so they sound positive.

Negative Word	Positive Word
Can't	*Can*
Won't	*Will*
I don't have enough money to travel	*I have plenty of money to travel*

Negative Word	Positive Word

Accountability

One thing I noticed about the successful people around me was that they always shared what they wanted. I believe a big part about manifestation and creating your dreams and goals is being able to share your thoughts and ideas with others, even if it might seem a bit uncomfortable.

#10 KimberTip: Listen to those you decide to share with. You may be surprised to receive some useful help and knowledge to move forward. Do you feel like your idea is real and very possible?

Activity #10 - Sharing your dreams

Make a list of all the people in your life who have helped you in the past. Beside their name write out how they impacted you. Use this list and call each one of them, sharing your future dreams and goals.

Family and friends can be very supportive if given the opportunity. Perhaps sharing your ideas will spark how they could help you NOW. And remember–dreams are possible.

Who will you share your goals and dreams with today? List 3 people.

1

2

3

Start journaling! Remember to use the 'Accomplishments Tracking Sheet' on page 250.

Are you stuck in an area of life? Which area? Write everything about it here:

Now write all the positive things about this area? What can you do differently? What new actions can you take?

Write down three goals. What do you want in life? Who do you want to be? Dream BIG! Even bigger than you think!

1

2

3

What did you learn today?

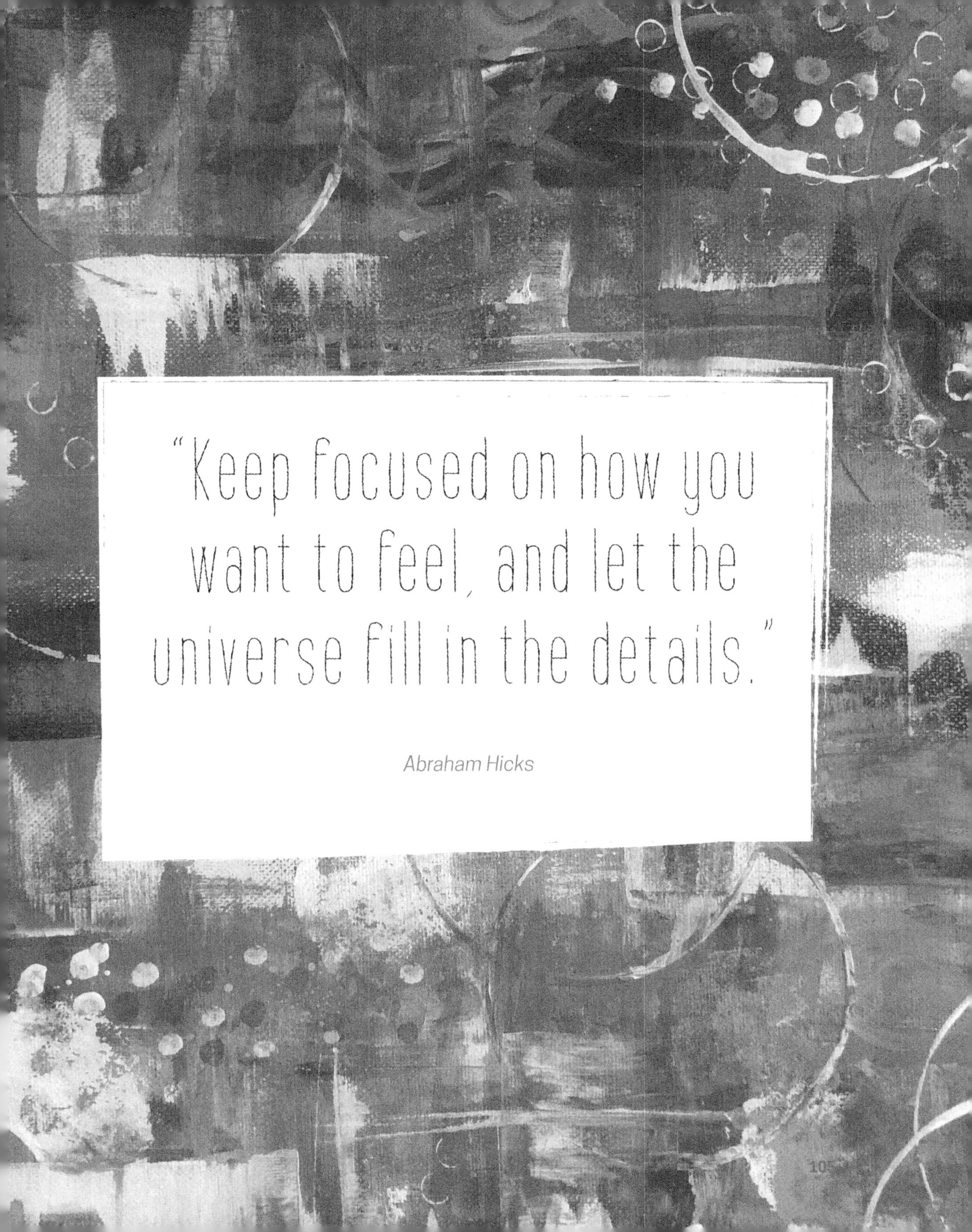
"Keep focused on how you want to feel, and let the universe fill in the details."
Abraham Hicks

What made you smile today?

Go back and look at your goals. What have you accomplished? Have you completed any of the goals? If not, write down your goals again. What actions will you take to move you closer to your goals? Write them here.

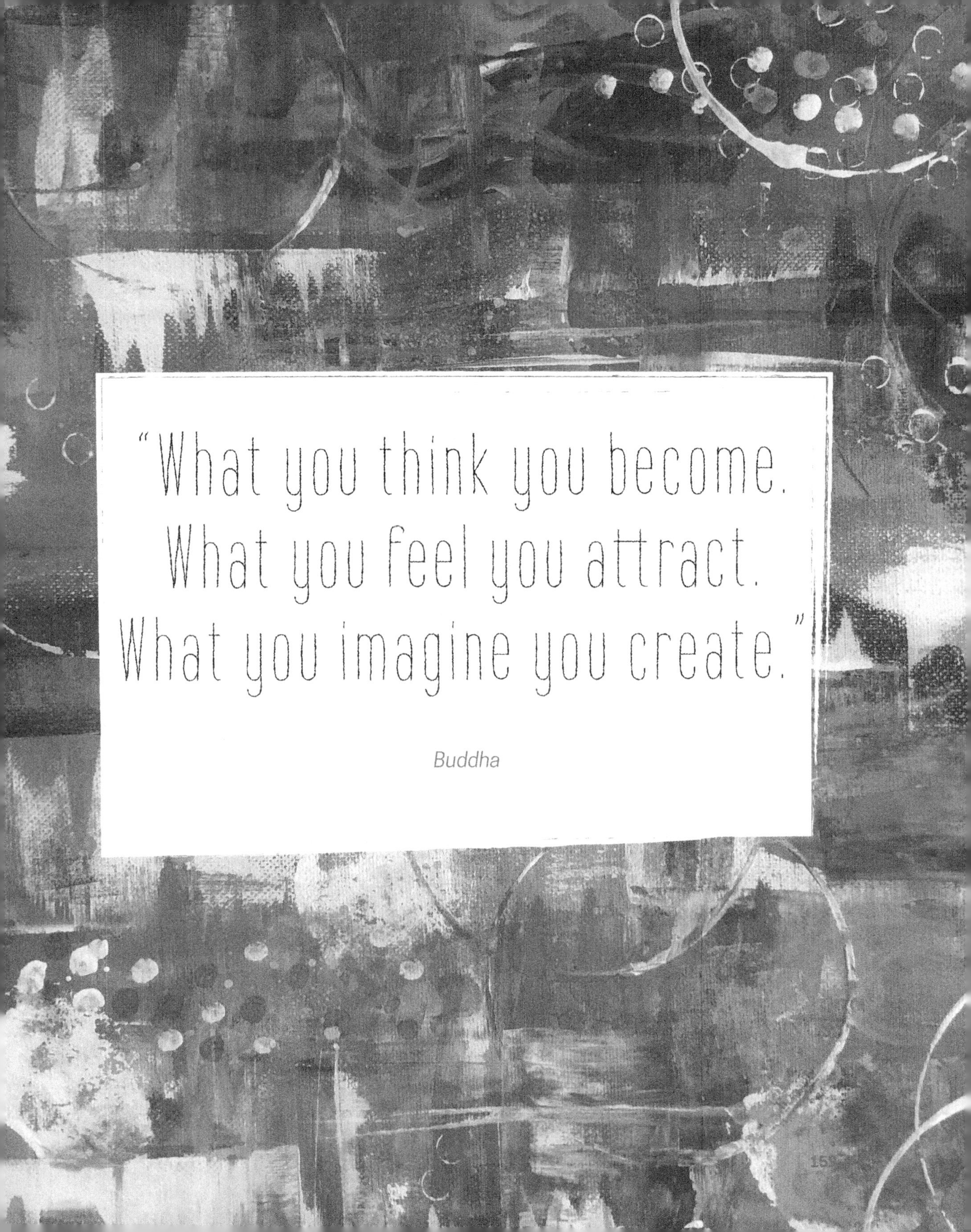
"What you think you become.
What you feel you attract.
What you imagine you create."
Buddha

Draw a picture of something you want. A new house...a new car...a picture of your future family... money... anything your heart desires!

Take a moment to review your entire journal. What did you discover? What do you still need to do?

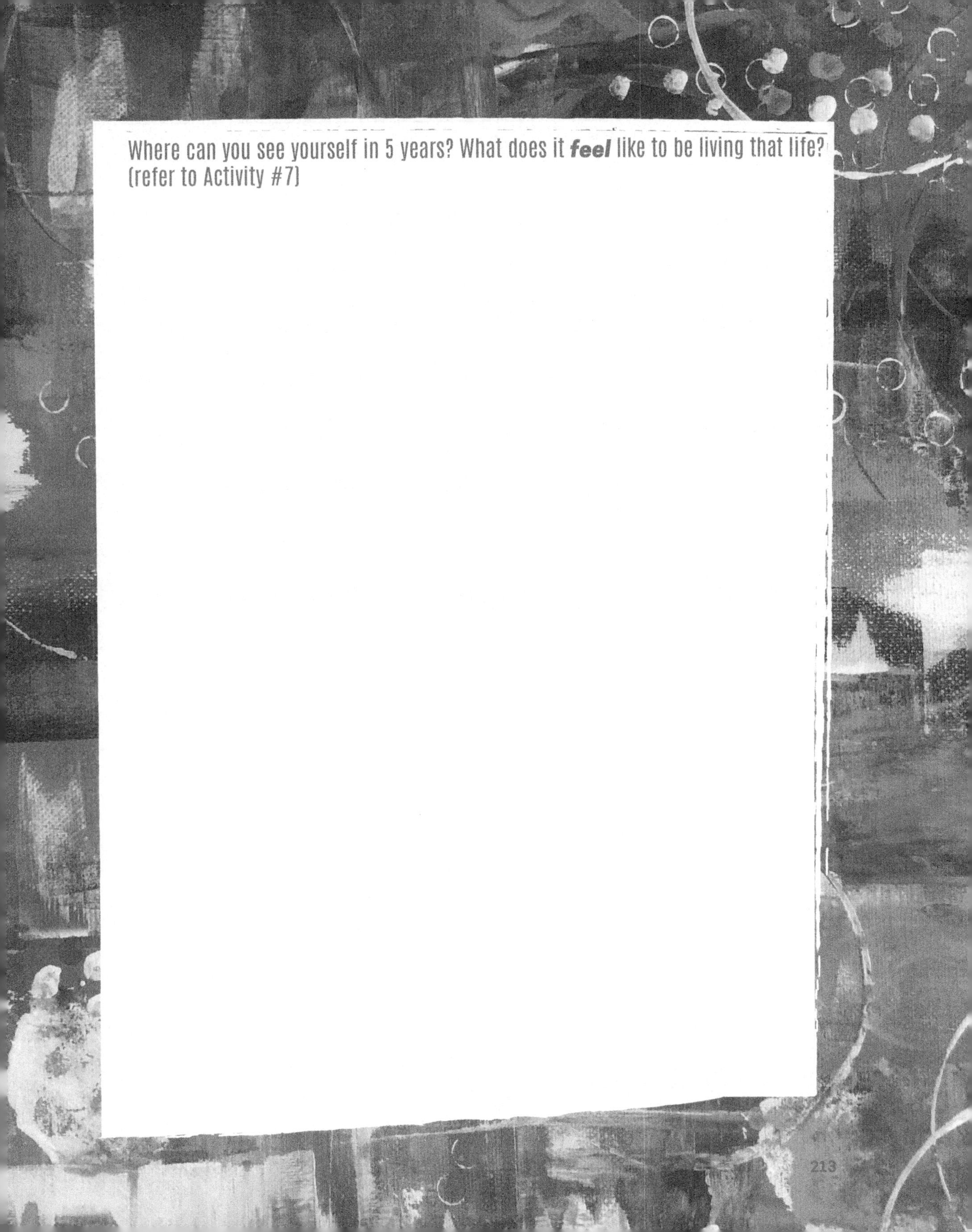

Where can you see yourself in 5 years? What does it ***feel*** like to be living that life? (refer to Activity #7)

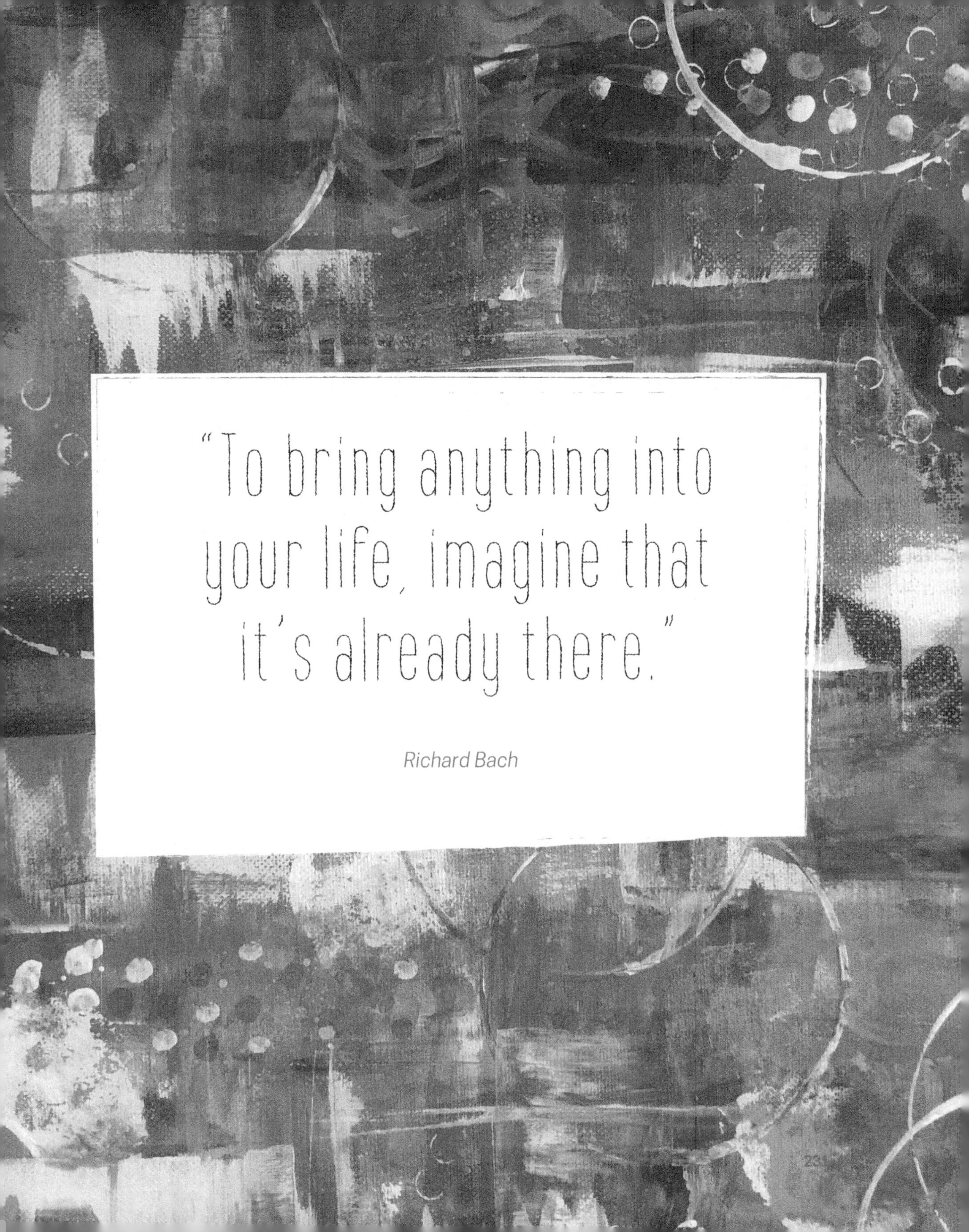
"To bring anything into your life, imagine that it's already there."
Richard Bach

What would you like to be acknowledged for today? Why?

Accomplishments Tracking Sheet

Activity #11 - What have you accomplished?

List all your accomplishments you have done over the course of journaling in this book. A way to check in to see if you are achieving your dreams and creating the life you want is by checking in. While you are using this journal & workbook, continue to write some of your accomplishments or breakthroughs you have had.

My Authentic Self

Coco and me

I inherited my creative skills and passion for the arts from both of my parents. As I grew I took a keen interest in watching my father work. When I was two years old, I thought I was such a big girl sitting at Dad's drafting table drawing with my paper and crayons beside him. I knew one day I would follow in his creative footsteps.

Over my teenage years, I continued to grow my imaginative skills, becoming more artistic and crafty, often making my own jewellery. I would make beaded jewellery and sell them to my family members, pretending I had my own business.

Visiting my grandparents was a weekly event. I would see my Grandmother's sewing table sitting along the far wall in the dining room. Often I would ask her questions about it and how it worked. One day my Grandma opened her closet and gave me a few of her patterns and sewing thread. Excited, I bought my own sewing machine and began sewing clothes from her gifted patterns. It was a new skill I had acquired and it felt quite amazing that I could make my own clothing for me and my friends.

"I believe creativity is an amazing skill to have."

During my 20's I decided I wanted to explore other ways to express myself. I enrolled and completed the Graphic Communications and Advertising diploma at George Brown College. I took a variety of courses including: life-drawing, computer, illustration and theory. All in support of expanding my career vision.

I now enjoy spending time crafting of original projects and selling them online. I also run a marketing company that provides marketing consulting and graphic design services.

In January 2018, through this book's **how-to of journaling**, I started a second company called Young at Heart Painting. This innovative art program for seniors provides an opportunity to learn how to paint. It's my honour and privilege to be working with seniors.

Presently, I help organizations across Canada and the United States create a productive work environment by providing meaningful, fun, art workshops.

My friends and family encouraged me to share my talents and skills with the world. Here I am!

To your future heart desires,

Kimberley Smith
Artist, Author & Consultant

Stay in touch!

Visit **www.kimberflydesign.com** to download a free workbook tool kit.

Facebook: **kimberflydesign**

Instagram: **@kimberflydesign**

kimberflydesign@gmail.com

Become a member! Be part of the journal club experience.
It's so easy at: **www.kimberflydesign.com**

Made in the USA
Middletown, DE
14 May 2021